Imagoes

Queer Anthology

J. Jones

ISBN: 1-7321532-4-8
ISBN-13: 978-2-7321532-4-0

DEDICATION

This book is dedicated to all the children who failed to identify as their gender birth only to find depression, abandonment and themselves at the light emitting from the end of the tunnel.

Table of Contents

Forward

In 2018, I sat down for an afternoon snack with Charles Stokes, founder of **Love Pain & Poetry**. It was during that conversation, that Charles proposed a, then burgeoning, concept for an anthology of queer poetry. Normally, I would scoff at such an idea being presented to me from a heterosexual publisher. I would be filled with concerns about what the larger intentions of the publisher were: profit from a specific market, perhaps? exploitation? tokenism - the ability to say "yes we've produced 'that' kind of work too"... the list goes on. And yet, my very necessary and very learned skepticism was quelled by the fact that, with this man, i formed a rather important bond. One that has gifted me with the knowing that his intention, and by extension- Love Pain & Poetry's intention, is to create a platform for the voices of those who, through the weight of marginalization, have been given eyes. Ferocious and intelligent eyes, with which to see the truth of existence. Thus, IMAGOES was born.

As the editor of IMAGOES, it has been my intention to answer three specific questions with the work found in this anthology: what work are we doing today? what is the importance or relevance of that work to the larger society? and how are queers naming themselves for themselves? The title IMAGOES can be defined as the sexual maturation stage in an insect's development: sometimes sprouting wings becoming fearsome and impressive, sometimes resulting in the defining or rejecting of a defined shape. The anthology also shares its name with two very important works to me, one by the poet Wanda Coleman and the other by fiction writer Octavia Butler. Both works deal with the complexities of developing an identity in the face of a crushing reality. The works, much like their namesake. ask us to interrogate a kind of creation narrative.

This collection defines itself as a queer anthology, meaning that each writer here identifies on a spectrum of sexuality, that in many ways is poorly defined. At the very least, each writer here has identified themselves as sexual minority. And while some work here touches on the sexual, it is not solely an exercise in pornography (although, we do like porn).

There is no way in which the work here could ever be singular in aim because that is not true of the lives of the contributors. As queer folk, we find ourselves at the intersections of sexuality, (dis)ability, race, gender and class. The work reflects that and pushes for a larger understanding of "queer" without pandering to ignorance. We encourage everyone (including those who do not identify as queer) to read this work because there are commonalities to be found in the emotion of the pieces. However we do not beg or hide ourselves for the sake of respectability.

In selecting the work to be featured in IMAGOES, I wanted to amplify the voices of emerging queers. The definition of "emerging" is often a thing of contention in the writing community. What distinguishes an emerging writer? At what point has one "emerged"? With the landscape of poetry being what it is (the marriages of publishing houses, clout economics, academia and questions of what makes a poem good enough to be printed) many poets find it difficult, if not impossible to be recognized for their brilliance. And many poets go unnoticed due to adversity and the very real inaccessibility of institutions. Yet, we are here. I am a member of community, at core. My career in poetry and writing, has been one of guerilla open mics, self published chapbooks, protest poems and community. In my work as an editor, i choose to honor that by amplifying the voices of others who are presenting work with teeth that tear at the institutional wheel.

Consider this: the first time I was accepted into a writing fellowship (The Watering Hole Poetry), my primary concern was whether or not I could stake claim to my space in such a place. I am, after all, an individual who does not hold an MFA, has not received a tremendous amounts of grants and publications and who does not claim to be able to "talk shop" in the most sophisticated of ways. What I brought to that fellowship, along with anxiety, was a hunger to create and to become better- to connect to community. What I found was an acceptance based on merit and desire. I found a space that afforded me the opportunity to be wholly myself and to learn alongside a group of skilled poets of varying backgrounds without the postural trappings that are sometimes present in these places. Spaces that do this work or healing and amplifying are critical. IMAGOES seeks to be such a space.

It is imperative that the work in this anthology be witnessed as a testament to the enduring power of the human will. The poems here deal with questions of ancestry, lust, vulgarity, mythology and joy. They are the fruit of writers who have spent years shaping their own narratives. It is with great pride that I present to you, IMAGOES, a queer anthology.

jamal rashad
Washington DC. 2019

jamal rashad

jamal rashad is a Black, a Queer, an optimist when careful, a massage therapist, and poet. He has received a fellowship from The Watering Hole Poetry. His work has been featured in Radar Productions, Maji Press, Argot Magazine, "Blackgirldangerous.com", the "Moonsalt" chapbook , and Against Equality. jamal as an editor for African Voices Magazine and currently works a poetry editor for Love, Pain & Poetry Publishing.

Untitled

a boy drowns in the river, which is flooding.

a boy maps out the change in currents.

boys, throwing bones in a courtyard, hear a person on the news speak about the boy who has drowned.

the boys, on a bus, read about the boy who has drowned.

the boys, who march, raise money for the families of other boys who have been taken under tow.

boys, with bloated skin, give lectures about the importance of reading moon charts.

a boy threatens to drown.

A boy cynicist, reads the skies and warns that there will be more drowning- silent, painful and slow.

boys become professional lifeguards.

near the gap, boys gather to make nice under trees, turn each other around and dance.

some boys lay wreaths.

a boy bathes himself in river water, finds the mouth and makes his bed.

A catalog of men

cotton plaid, short sleeve. Target pink and green.
red bull and hashish. Preston. wide grinning, flat nose.
those greedy brown eyes. 20.00
came crooning one Berkley night. gave me my first full gut.

crisp ironed, deep blue slacks. contrary dashiki red.
locs dipped in coconut oil.big black man hands. wide set Stacy
Adams size 11
on that bike we liked to call Negro Sunshine. 16.00 Marcus. always
gave me permission to moan.
he always promised to clean up when he came on my back.

black colored thief's hoodie. nondescript sweat bottom. same
black.
Steven. missing molars covered with a wild man's tongue.
he'd breathe into every curve 17.50. eyes set on somewhere south.
come jumping in that beat up Dodge Ram. come jumping with that
missing rear view.
coke boogers hanging. when he came up he'd always beg to be let
in.

solid. stout. size 36. Kenneth. in navy blue boxers and copper skin.
wide chest with bashful hair. plucked brows modest. Nike slippers
well worn
housing his unkempt feet. my thighs shaking on his boulder
shoulders
him humming old soul while he ate. 25.00. left me empty when he
came up.

Tarvar. sweet silly smiling boy. brown eyes all of 23. child like his
happy trail turned to wonder.

said i was the first punk he ever "stuck". 10 inch dirt road stroke.
rattle my home. brown loafers.
caught the 92 to my house. cheery lollipop sweet tooth. 15.00.
fingers always came to pinch my meat as we rode round town.

navy green cargo pants. gray turtle neck. ganja smoke clouding up
his nightly news.
ganja smoke clouding a single crucifix on his wall. Larry. held me
close on his almond chest.
nipples hot wired to his cock. not one for straight talk. marble eyes
rolled straight to my heart.
eyes gone deliberately blind when i needed seeing. 17.25.
"babe, I got someone out of town. I need a boy to come to when
im down here."

Scene 26

I.

In the hallway. naked.
He bends down to milk the bull.
I stumble into his throat.
Against the wall, we become one.
Inseparable.
Glued in his grip.

II.

In the shower. Steam.
I fall onto him.
In his eyes I see myself.
Jump.
Tiring now, in this ritual - dance.
Im stuck as he cups and squeezes
one last time.

III.

In the bed, he finds my thigh-
a meaty pillow.
two fingers pinch my flesh.
wrap around my skin.
One creeps to meet my wet mouth.
He's at home, my man,
settling down.
sighing
"sweet baby you taste so good"

Two Dog Life

We suffer cold
lying down.
bound by frost
and silence, broken by occasional rhythmless clunks of sound.
sex comes in abundance or not at all.

We touch.
Skin sticks,
freezing in this old ice box of wood and no spigot.
The driptray's gone the same way of my voice.

We'd rather be elsewhere.
He shakes himself off first
And finds his way out.
Im stuck here.
With the mattress,
some pill scripts for diagnosis,
the worry.

Too chilled to cry.
Too bit to move.
Wish there was something else I could put on.

Single Room Occupancy
After Wanda Coleman

The mold on my windowsill is conspiring against me to form a union
with the fungi on my sheet thin mattress and my neighbor tells me

with a full chest/ eyes swimming in water, that he is sending off
to Africa for a bride and ask what i think is a fair price

music is the slow drag of the mules at 6 am headed to pasture
only giving pause for the widow, on the other side of me, whos still
screaming

about 1992 and the mice we both hear at dawn, living defiantly
has brought me solitude in a room, in neutral, in a shack

squat , in this gray struck place and slumped
on this cushionless pastel chair where i cover the chipped paint of the
walls

with what art a week of sucks on unemployment can buy-
my thighs have been without moisture for months

and now the only comforts i have are in the thousands of trite little
verses i manage to write monthly, hoping to strike gold

there is a man in philadelphia who has hexed me and try as i might
I can't seem to keep the weight off

home is unmonitored doses of sleeping pills to silence
the mariachi coming from two flights down

i'm on the 5th floor and home is the light on the phone telling me
that the sender, somewhere, has some good dirt to share

sometimes i sleep in the same outfit twice hoping it will look just as good
tmrw

since my money is scarce and i can't always drop quarters at the laundromat

sometimes i sleep for days and wake up missing things i can't remember appointments for stamps, case worker visits, inspection dates.

sometimes I startle awake from my nap, feet slapping the floor looking in the mirror, after i've done a once over and counted where them bugs done bit.

"...least I still got my eyes."

12 Ways of Looking at a Nightbird

i.

four centuries of wading
the only movement backwards
is the rushing tide to strike red.

ii.

i am splayed
against the ugliness of my own mythologies
the cries of civilized conversation
in civilized society lost
in this hour of gnashing teeth.

iii.

i saw a vamp
in his cadillac coupe' de ville
and knocked seven times on the lamp post for luck.

iv.

when windows are boarded shut
they dizzy and dim the red glare
of a coming July.
still pockets of glow indicate
where we are in this breathless squat.

v.

the only true marriage
my mother says a boy child can have
is the one between him and the lips
that birthed him. the only one i know
is the orgy of she, i and the deathstone.

vi.

when the cops came, they didn't knock
but three of us down and charged
the john an inconvenience fee
for wasting their time.

vii.

and the men got rich off of
latex and bo' and the back alley owls
took their own ears to spite
the deafening jabber of parades.

viii.

of the white men who have lusted for me
i do not know which i prefer
the beauty of contaminants
the beauty of silence
or what came before.

ix.

we oiled in the abandominium
while they danced
between sucks he looked at me
"dont you sometimes want to be like them?"

x.

when he came he promised me
the moon and the stars
when he split
all he left was stars

xi.

when i kicked and put on the weight
no one told me
about the groove it'd leave
in park benches.

xii.

struck mad from a chemical whirling
i awoke in the inpatient
flanked by clipboards and labcoats screaming:

"they will not be saviors, no!
they will not come, on horseback, at high noon, no!
they will not even be poets."

Lauren Bullock

Lauren Bullock is a queer Black and Vietnamese writer, performer, and teaching artist. Her work has appeared on AFROPUNK.com, Button Poetry, Thank You For Swallowing, and more. Currently she serves as a staff writer for pop culture website Black Nerd Problems as well as poetry editor for literary magazine FreezeRay Poetry. When not working on writing-related activities she enjoys fighting crime as a costumed vigilante of many aliases.

Suppose your neck is where my love lies

somewhere between the sweet ropes
of your hair, an inch or so before your
shoulder's flat plane smooths to a jaw.
There, soft as a kiss, cold water fetched
in mason jars, a night illuminated with
coals and smoke, arguing domestically
about the beads and the ironing, yes,
the lazy drape of your arm and the insistent
sun, a mistaken toothpick, a bite of potato
too much, the morning walk and its sudden
song. And do you carry it knowingly? With
care or as a shameful secret, a festering
rash? Before sleep, does your partner
brush it with her fingers, sigh at another
tattoo?

Go

(an erasure of "Tango: Maureen" from Jonathan Larson's RENT)

Mark, I told her that I'm here
to wait. She's the delay,
the test. Anything but fuckin'
I do, fighting my bones like a fire,
drinking a honey she keeps dangling.
She is different with me and you
turn cold. I think I know her lips' call.
Have you ever walked so cautious?
I'm in her room and it's hard to do this,
cheat. Heated up right now. Look with
all of your might for her still dance.
You don't grip. You think, "Might at least
pretend to believe her cause in the end."
You can't end it. You till and turn love
obscene. Try. You know now you never forget.

Princess Bubblegum and Homura Akemi Advising the Author on Worldbuilding

Let's say you're granted the chance
to convert the world's grief to candy, an
unfathomably easy chemistry
when you consider how long you've
been sketching this formula's skeleton.
And even when they do
succumb finally, by choice,
the idea of this best friend embracing
the curse you both ought to confront
is too distant a sadness to grasp
when the syrup starts sticking to your brain.
You sing *let me call you sweetheart*
trying to end to no avail. The thoughts keep
dissolving into sugar, an appetizing mess.
Somewhere in the stream floats
the image of the person you were before.
You know
you can't recognize their laughter
because you'd rather be swallowed
by forgetting.
Your not-quite-lover will leave
easily.
Yourself
to backwards
you confuse sweetness,
conformity, and comfort
yourself with
tower of
ink melting.
You recall their hair smelling exactly of
campfire.
Only now, after all you have made
sweeter
do you realize
you can't even remember why you loved them.

To change the universal laws and live
or, more accurately, dream. The craft
too subtle for praise but you still
tried to make your beloved understand
anyways for when God has their bad days.
You can't help what wounds you leave,
are vulnerable to.
You and all your faults
so simply erased from memory
with just your two soft hands
pulling. It feels like what they said they wanted but
crueler. A version your friends continue
infiltrating: first, your body as a tomb, then
the whole fabric of being stretched bizarrely. Their name
is the only thing tying you here.
Better
becoming destruction
than allowing a red inch of regret to bloom.
You permit this to happen knowing one day
they might even hate you but at least
for the moment you strip
all the clocks of truth, are
clinging to pretend. You're losing sense
and sincerity, change and progress.
If entropy is inevitable then what kind of
time, stretched thin as
desire, can hold you two together?
On the inside of your chest it feels like
incense
lit the last time you held them, smoldering still.
Love to
you takes the shape of a frightening color
that no one else can comprehend
but you do.

Need a larger Font?

Scan me

this morning i re(-)collect the sky

                                                  planet's shift paring life down
                                                  to quiddity &

quiet pleasant with petrichor or
                            liquid   spilling a hymn through the cherry
leaves

before a downpour swings loose
                      the fruit buds now smothered

the memory of my cheek cradled
                            in tender umber cannot resurface

from the warm berth   i (re)turn
                                              to metamorphosis

to that juvenescent slope & our
                      bed darkened with the almost

    eager skein of skin   i say i am
        eroding the roots of this paradisaic garden

    comfortable with my choice
                            to shed

that summer you became lost
                                      any muddy burdens   & leave
                                      behind growth

Troy Oko

Troy Oko (Troy Rockett), a non-binary actor, first discovered performance through poetry where she embodied the genre to empower herself: a Black Queer adoptee. Troy Oko is a VONA/Voices Fellow and Astraea Lesbian Writers' grant recipient and holds a joint MA degree in Creative Writing and Literature from Holy Names University. Her poems are included in Best New African Poets Anthology 2017, Chorus: A Literary Mixtape, Sinister Wisdom 106: The Lesbian Body, CALYX, Q-Zine, and Bay area based projects, Bay Area Generations and Nomadic Press' Get Lit. She acts with local theatre companies in the Bay Area and collaborates with queer storytellers on independent film projects.

lover

You fit my bed   better than my sheets
smelling of deep steeped tea and coconut flesh
crown of braided locks,
                          willow roots rusted in moss

Can I kiss you   there,   along the hairline
where   manicured   meets   fuss?

armor

Don't act like you know this body
I go days without   breathing
my gender   is an open wound
I go through   days bleeding
Don't act like you.   know nature
half of my body   hunts the other
the other wears   death flaunting
I know hunger   I have its teeth
          around my neck
   I have it being rammed inside
I have you asking me once again
        to explain   why I'm here
and why like this.   When
everything I walked here with   is
habitat and survival.

here

meet people and ask their names
ask can you *show me how to deal*
with living?
laugh when you are meant to faint
ok ok. there's green bananas
in the bright bowl. and your friend's
voice is medicine you can slip into
your ears through the cracked phone.
ok. and there's a bag of salt
and water that can grow hot
there are many ways to pray
ok palms. ok tummy roll and sweet
meat between thighs as you bend
lower your head for the first time today
repeat. *I'm here   I'm ok.*

ghostmen

1.

I feel as if a ghost
the ones looking can't see what I am
that I once grew wild
now life and light have made me still

here each limb becomes a stranded stem
my mountains dug out from underneath:
a fort for my protection
there are now more holes in me than dreams

2.

This body is my only reward after the war
I am in a bed of scar tissue blooming
I think of the beach where sand castles
made from similar surgeries
must now appear as ocean filled wounds

my lover my gardener
you've made it your job to mind these mines
you place your head, ear to this battlefield
your fingers tease the barbed wires where
we walk and love as wars do

as it is

                    I often think of you   and
every face that turns
            I find myself   still looking
for the then unmarried woman   who
dared   traverse   the landscape
of a body   unlike and like her own.

For first times and harnessed truths
     for those we burned
                  in our bending of tradition
       for the sun who held her tongue
to the night
who sang into our dreaming   let us
always wake   knowing ourselves.

I love our **contemplating** of the body

There. I told the surgeon. *I won't let anyone make this body*

            a cage
and off the two breasts went   flying without wings

I believed hands could gift me flight
      and now my fluid is a jagged scar
          chained to my
        chest.
"Trans?" or "Real?"
I won't pick every bone from my body just to slide
        through your teeth more easily.

Every word strikes a hammer against this hot iron
do you have what you thought you needed
just say *goodbye* like you mean it
then escape or landscape or risk being a scapegoat

    a fire forested of toes gone uprooted from spring
    a horizon I could never reach

Set here while I darken this becoming is bone breaking
or a fish market, where I come head-wrapped and headless

So now, *no,* I don't want anyone

          to come back for me
       I'm gone

I kept breathing out tongues
they left and split into hissing kissing summer rain
        won't last

Here.   I made my chest a cleared field for landing
a horizon I can always reach

Juanita!   she's my country, my heart

       I'm country at heart
       I'm this country at heart
       This country stole my granny's heart

I'm her *apology* for this madness.

My favorite flower in bloom: Myn
PART 1: 1 am @ (The People Party) 2013

I am
Taking up this space
66 inches tall
spreading wingspan to take you in
blow by blow
whack by whack
body roll and neck snap

at the end of the set, house is now dub, 74 inches of you
steps into this space
hand on hip you are a question mark before me.
you ask "What do you prefer?"

I prefer: feminists, spiritualists, socialists, art enthusiasts
the list could go on
but for the sake of time
I prefer you. I prefer this right now.
your shea butter with hint of lavender.
chapstick thickly applied.
morning dew visiting your skin on this night groove.
clinging fabric to muscle tone.
this dimly lit cavern dressing your copper tone.

How I would love to undress you as the sunrise undresses the
night
But you were only referring to the music when you asked my
preference

you take my assumption as compliment
your body smiles off to some other corner
a languid switch in your narrow hips.

I am left back hung against wall considering my cockiness.

PART 2: 2:15 am (Unlocking Bikes)

74inches is unlocking hys bike
two metal rings away from me

two firm cheeks pressed into a tight bud
    now spreading to bear the mouth of hys entrance

        What I would do if I had all my parts
        I would fit myself deep into that opening

        I fit key into lock
        and rack my brain for some one liner
                                or an   appropriate
way to invite someone over for the night

        hy straddles his bike
        Hey!rides out of my mouth before he can take off
        Which way are you riding? "Laurel District"
        Mental Math prompts invitation
        I tell hym I'm just up the street
                                        Let

us pretend I had all my parts...

PART 3: (Outline)

No trace of love
as mouth tongue and teeth
search the stencil of hym
fitting my bed better
than my sheets.

Hys eyes trace the stencil of me
no masculine tailored cut
to conceal curves
my free form
is something hy is not familiar with.

I am missing part of speech
and cannot fill hys mouth and throat
like I want to

What my stencil lacks I make up in freehand
free hand curves the direction of hys vowel.

The length of hym curves to the left
we curve into Cs
and we are cursive on sheet
we are mouthfuls broken into curse
words.

between the lines of hym smooth and
fluid
unedited I will not tell you where hym or I
put it
or where we indented
or who was the heading

We are finished
assignments
we turn ourselves in
 unstapled, unbound, lacking covers

Morning will look us over

through slanted glass
and mark us
passing grades

There will be a trace of love

sweat stenciled into sheet
where we labored over
alphabet
and made sense of my
missing vowel
and sometimes Y
and sometimes Y
is not required to be a man.

.

A.M. Hemingway

A.M. Hemingway is a writer and poet. Born in 1991, Hemingway has read their poetry in intimate settings since 2011. In 2011, they founded the short-lived Black Thought, a literary blog, and served as its editor-in-chief. Hemingway studied English Literature and has assembled a chapbook, 'Dreams of Being a Disembodied Black Person' (self-published, 2017). Hemingway's poetry often serve as elegies for lost moments and loved ones; their short stories use unreliable narrators and center on nonlinear narratives and simulated reality. Hemingway lives in Columbus, Ohio, and is working on their first full collection.

The Dream as a Silent Film I Have Never Seen, In a Foreign Language

There
used to be
a boy. What
used to be
a boy would
sit in parked
cars and think
about what
used to be.

Two people
used to be
closer, a man
and what
used to be
a boy. One
said something to
the other. What
was said was
lost.

The rain
used to bring
comfort. The rain,
never concerned with
what it means
to be, falls.
The sky is
cloudy now, but
there is no
rain.

Two people
used to be
closer, a man
and what
used to be
a boy. One
attempted to teach
the other how
to wear a
hijab. What was
taught was just
a dream.

This space
used to be
empty, or maybe
quieter.
Then life happened.

Two people
used to be
closer, a man
and what
used to be
a boy. One
stood and smoked.
What the moment
means, no one
knows.

The boy,
or what
used to be,
now through with
thinking, goes back
to what they
    used to do.

Two Ghosts Stories

Colors and I took a
seat on the corner of
East 6th Avenue and Summit
Street. I opened a bottle
of Sailor Jerry and took
my fourth gulp of rum.
Colors was not the old
man's name. He shrugged. Cars
passed by me. I lit
another cigarette and continued drinking
    alone

Olympus, the House You Once Owned

you once owned a house
with two marble pillars and
three brass doors you owned
this house and nothing else
from wall to wall and
from floor to ceiling sat
stood existed nothing at night
lights built into the porch
would introduce the house to
darkness and you would sit
across the street smoking a
cigarette in fear watching the
lights turn your house your
home your monument into a
mausoleum this was before the
cut on your left middle
finger this is no longer
this was back then this
was back when you owned
    the house

Some Voyage of Former Selves

Your former self
used to go deep
into wooded areas
to find the lost
objects and places
people and time
had forgotten. When
you found the forgotten
places you found
nothing was as it
seemed and people
were not who they
claimed to be. It
would rain, and
now when it rains
you feel a feeling
you cannot describe
with this heavy,
foreign, mechanical
language. You found
the forgotten places
and what other people
had forgotten. You
did not find what
you had forgotten.
Nowadays you encounter
past lives but no
wooded areas. Plenty
of clouds but no
rain. Years have
passed and at times
you saw your former
selves flicker across
your vision. Different
parts of the past

in a present superposition.
You remembered when
this lake was different,
when it meant more
than it does now,
more than it ever
could again. You
remembered how she
smiled, and ached
in quiet places
when you could not
see it, because
you could see it
everywhere. You
wondered where you
went wrong but there
was no right and
what was left was
the running faucet
of doubt. At the
lake you caught
a glimpse of yourself
losing yourself
in your self-pity.
Night fell and you
stumbled with a
gasoline stink fresh
on your hands. Somewhere
your old home turned
to cinders. Your
former self staggered
back to where you
live now, met you
in the mirror, and
begged you to dream.
Under moonlight,
the two of you became
one pulse. Now you

are alone and think
about your past
selves. Dream and
see the man who
died so long ago.
You did what you
did to forget he
was ever here. Streetlights
turn people into
shadows. The shadows
stretch across the
lake. Some of the
shadows stop to
observe spooky action
at a distance. You,
however, close your
eyes and see the

    same house in flames.

Haunted

Take on the unconscious wandering of another and trace every
moan back to the original thought. When opening the eyes,
gaze into the abyss of someone unknown. When known,
you see someone who has lost. Someone who
has lost loss. Who has gained more.
Lost again, gained less. Scrounged what
was left. Saved bits and
pieces. Budgeted love. Spent
nights. In the
morning, awoke
Broke.

Tuskegee, In a Period of Darkness

Sit in a parked
car. Stare at the
old home of a
lost loved one. Do
not exit the vehicle
this time. Leave for
more alcohol. Drive by
a dilapidated Hunt Brother's.
Reflect on a faded
memory. Repeat.

S. Shaw

is a poetry and fiction writer who has attended writing conferences in various African nations. His poems have been published in African American Review, Temenos Literary Journal, The Missing Slate, as well as a short story in Mighty Real: An Anthology of African American Same Gender Loving Writing. He is a Cave Canem Poetry Fellow. He has a chapbook titled The House of Men from Glass Lyre Press.

How Come Me Here

A poem in retrograde

1-
Her bosom is softer than cotton
I call it home during resting time
When work is done and chores forgotten

After I bring the wash within
Moments between work, lay down and climb up
Her bosom is softer than cotton

In these moments I know my life is not for nothing
When she speaks all the words rhyme
When work is done and chores forgotten

Mornings come hard and rotten
No time to tarry or look behind
But her bosom is softer than cotton

Days we say bye to our begotten
Push the taste of their smiles from mind
'Til when work is done and chores forgotten

The track from home is worn and well-trodden
Her hidden kiss sublime
Her bosom is softer than cotton
When work is done and chores forgotten

2-
Cotton cotton cotton
Forgotten

Her body   works
Brings in the wash   works
Chop da cotton

Her bosom   work
Her bosom   soft

IMAGOES

Her bosom is resting time

I walk the path
To her bosom
Soft soft soft

I will tarry
Look behind for her track
Follow it back to her

My begotten are sublime
Her bosom
Cotton

Bosom bosom bosom
Soft. Cotton

I am forgotten
Work and chores
Forgotten. My begotten
Are soft
Her words rhyme
Her bosom
Is soft.

3-
It is rotten   my bosom.
I say goodbye
Begotten, cotton
Soft her bosom

Go Down Moses

I am tumble
I am ground I

Am down
I am earth.

Ginger root
dig and dug

The hollow left
the spaces nothing settles in

I am outside in rain
Watered dust

I am child
Run jump

Hide and seek
sometimes find

I am the desire
The call   the response

I am the names
Crucified on my tongue

The black splinter
Left beneath his skin

I am child
Grown too soon

The grieving beard
Spilling hosannas

I am stories
unrequited love

I am the black splinter left
Between his quaking thighs

The amen whispered – eyelids kissed
When no one is looking

When solace is a long way off
In green rows of cotton tobacco, corn

I am touch – the hide and seek,
the finding

The crucifixion to desire
When home is long lost.

Rock-a-my Soul

It is Monday or Sunday
It is church   he

Is prayer and
Prayed up

He is on the cross
Moaning   he

Is the cross when morning
Comes and   he

Is a moaning green
Willow tree

He is swaying "oh..
father, do not. OH"

He prays to strong hands
That lay down vespers

Vine through his
Dark moments and sprout

He does not want
Death to be his safe space or

His keeping place
His place of sanctuary

In the fields
Pick one, pick two, pick forever

He listens to the other men

IMAGOES

Pray for salvation and release

He is surrounded by the calls and cries
He is unending in his rocking

He is the call
The response

He is relentless
in his soul-stirring.

Roll Jordan Roll

When morning falls from his mouth. It
is beautiful. The
Cotton blossom's tumble
Not so onerous,
So thorny when
he brings them to be weighed.

I walk the waters, cross the waves,
Forget my yoke
When he calls my name.

Sweet Chariot

Somewhere behind in left out memories, is the father
Father of the son left behind in acidic darkness, left
Behind to tell of how life was,
Should be. Behind the woman's back
He speaks of the father, behind
The house, behind in the overgrown yard
He plays w/other
Left behind boys, he plays
He is the left behind
Father, becomes
Oracle creating a world
From left behind memories.

The left behind mother is not
The father does not know what
Being left behind
Feels like for the son, does not know what leaving
A father behind does to a son. The woman behind a closed smile
Does not see her son twist and hang
Like a long day behind in its divinity; behind
In its duty to be day, behind in calling to the wind
To sweep away the evening. The son
Does not see the left behind woman
Looking for her glory – *Get thee behind me*
Satan, she says, dragging her other kids
From behind her skirts. Swinging
Low to catch her fall.

WADE IN THE WATER

When he was tossed
Over, he smelled
Of my blood. A splintered pinky swear, a
Blood oath, a frantic
kiss. The beasts
came – unhoused him from his flesh
ate him
Bit
by
bit.
His hands, that were never
Empty of mine, that
Clustered around my wrists
Like manacles.
His legs that swayed
With the waters roll, his
Tongue that spoke my name, that
Called his mama, his people
Pushing them deep into me, invading
Cracks opened and ragged
From raw planks. All gone.

The sharks were not picky
Did not discriminate between
Man or woman,
The cardinal angle of a body in dispossession.
Blood
Was blood. Mine
Drew them to him. They
Ate of us both. But
His manhood lay upon
The waters black and slick, his
Dick buoyed
intact in the waves. Mine,
lengthened

In farewell.

Olokun, has crossed him over, God
Has troubled the waters.

Ciara Swan

Ciara Swan is a multimedia artist from Oakland California.
Through poetry, Swan attempts to create textual maps that provide
a visual and literary structure for each message.

N9NE Lives

Fact of the matter, they splatter   then scatter
Remnants of power,
           those who have it never chatter,
           symbolism embedded in this cursed language

I   opt to wisely choose words,
           pardon my mutable energy-   these days
I'm constructing worlds in body language

Hump
     then dump thee,
   walls stacked

Don't have the courage   to

           fall-

that's what I call an

           ovulating integrity-

I'll mind fuck you instead
     Mental is packing a machine gun
          Clap Brah- rah tah ou we
            Bellies ache
            when the eyes too big for taste

            Swine stained;
slow and steady our organs they're tryna slang

           Survival tactics to keep us ill fit in their
Black Market

(Free game) check to a mate who tryna pass the Dutch –
            foreign waters never looked
          so tempting –

           empty the glass til its
50/50
     My cup runneth

Crescendo (cursive tongues)

In an age of opportunity, I Opt poor unities, which catalyst
foundations of <-Aa-P.O.C.-a-
    lip-tick->
        memory foam brains that cave under pressure; forming plush
      shores of   synthetic plasticity:
  Ride
            the waves of
    hands whose palms house stale soul ties and wonder why I got
    low
    energy

Remember me, blaq? That séance naga who conjured ancestors to see
the answers in every jointed spliff and bottled bliss throwing up tests
from my intestines to practice a dim witted glory. Aint no fury, trying
to (posit+) some foresight so I can re-write our story

Hours; the time flowers in porcelain pots, all towering their highest to
the sun/
no more heroes they ramble while their faces mold to heru, planted in
herut
      Her root
            aint ever failed to supply.

Supple scorning can make skins cry; we call it sweat.
Attention spans/
      im   moving   fast,
         she   calls it   neglect-
                     trigger   isms to
reconfigure trauma
                           collects'
   like

Calling collect, you paid for your life lesson to repeat itself...
 Higher learning mollifying the outcome/ appeasing what be
 Higher learning nullifying the outcome/ disregarding what be
    Its scary when only two letters can change a meaning

Dena Rod

Dena Rod is a writer, editor, and poet based in the Bay Area. A graduate of San Francisco State University, they have a M.A. in English Literature. They are currently the managing editor of Argot Literary Magazine, a queer non-profit with a mission to highlight and sponsor LGBQTIAA+ perspectives and art across the globe. Through creative nonfiction essays and poetry, Dena works to illuminate their diasporic experiences of Iranian American heritage and queer identity, combating negative stereotypes of their intersecting identities in the mainstream media.

Hadith / Traditions for the Closet

A is for Ahmadinejad, stands and claims "In Iran, we don't have homosexuals." What he means is in America, we come out to our families. Yet in Iran, we don't burden our families with this knowledge. Gay liberation is a Western phenomenon whereas gay acts are universal.

A is for *Amrad*, Persian for the beardless youth of male beauty. Hurled towards a person who engages in homosexual acts.

A is for Ali A, publicly hanged and executed for suspected homosexuality in 2005 at Gorgan, a northern Iranian town and buried in an unmarked grave.

A is for Asylum, denied to those Muslims quagmired in Turkey, deprived of safety and exiled from their homelands.

B is for Ban, upheld by the U.S. Supreme Court. We won't let any Muslims, Venezuelans, or North Koreans inside.

B is for *Birooni*, outsiders looking in, bordered and crowding the queer internet for a sense of belonging and community.

B is for Barbaric, what the West thinks of Iran, a bitter legacy held well over fifty years.

C is for Coming Out, an American invention imported.

C is for Contradictions, kissing men on each cheek but never on the lips. You can engage in the act but deflect from identity.

D is for *Dabbab*, Persian for crawling over, over the gentle slope of your broken down back,

D is for Double Life, as long as you Don't Ask and Don't Tell, your family will tolerate you

D is for Disowned if you don't.

D is for Dyke, a word that has no equivalent in Persian.

D is for Death threats, what awaits you back home for when you come out abroad.

E is for Exile, because if you come out of the closet, there go your family, your friends, the social death branded upon your honor.

E is for Execution, not limited to political dissidents, Shah supporters, or transgressive women.

E is for Extermination, the sour slaughter of countless Iranian gays for indulging in their "satanic urges"

F is for Firing Squad, crouched down and aimed forward with their rifles straight. F is for Fundamentalist, the strain of Islam now rooted in Iran for almost forty years

G is for *Gulam-pare*, Persian for boy ravisher. Once a rite of passage into manhood, yet if you ravish too much, you risk becoming the ravished.

H is for *Hasha*, Persian for denial, pushing away this something outside of Iranian culture.
H is for Hostage: while there were lesbians drinking at Maud's and Amelia's in San Francisco, there were American hostages in Iran
H is for Homosexual Genocide, an extermination campaign headed by the state, hidden from international view until 1990. Eleven years of death, swept away.

I is for Islamic Revolution, a theocratic regime democratically voted into power.
I is for Inflict. Stand the condemned straight, slice in two with a sword, then behead while positioned with legs apart. Once the corpse falls down, set fire and burn to ashes. Or to save time, dig a hole. Set the homosexual on fire and throw them in the hole. I is for Ignored

J is for Justice, the judge's choice. Beheading by sword, stoned to death, thrown from a mountain, murdered under the rubble of a wall demolished on your head, or simply burned alive. J is for Joon, the spirit, the soul, the life stripped away

K is for *Koshkesh*, Persian for "procurer of pussy," ladies smoking cigarettes to signal to the men on the street.
K is for *Kunkesh*, the procurer of ass, clean-shaven men in tight pants, with clutch purses held tightly in the crook of their arms

L is for *Lavat*, the Persian word for sodomy, punishable by death L is for the lashes I would receive for kissing my wife

L is for the longing inside to see the mountain I'm named after. Yet with every word I write, the chasm between that dream and reality widen.

M is for Maryam Khatoon Molkara, the first trans women in Iran who paved the way for those behind her.
M is for *Mosaheqeh*,lesbianism.
M is for Mercy, none extended when the state decides you are a criminal for where your genitals touched.
M is for *Marg bar Āmrikā*, Death to America, or rather Death to American policies, sanctions, and state-authorized coups.

N is for Neighbors who could be snooping on you, and report your activities
N is for Nuclear, Iran's first program to enrich uranium co-sponsored by the United States in the 1950s. Now we withdraw and we sanction.

O is for Outsider, as I linger on the fringe, Farsi rusting on my tongue, struggling to find the
narratives of other queer Iranians
O is for Ostracized
O is for Overdue

P is for Purge, an exercise in futility as seeds of dissent planted between landmines still buried in Abadan.
P is for Persian, not Iranian, conjuring up exotic images of cats and carpets.

Q is for Queer, a word that has no translation in Persian

R is for Repressed, the inability to write "LGBT refugee" on your asylum application because
then they'll know. Everyone will know.
R is for Regime, rooted for forty years.
R is for Religion, the cross-pollination of Christianity to Islam passing on the Biblical judgment for same-sex acts.

S is for Shahid - bazi,witnessing boys' beauty, for if boys weren't witnessed did they exist?

S is for Sufis, those who observed boys' beauty in verse, in the worship of Allah, persecuted by
S is for the Secret Police, who may be lurking around any corner to catch you, report you, put
you on trial, in jail, and in a noose.
S is for Shame.

T is for Tusahiq, having sex with other women.
T is for Tafkhiz, defined as frottage.
T is for Taboo
T is for Tashakor, Gratitude, I am thankful for my birth in this country.

U is for Underground, where the queer community is, hidden from prying eyes in Shiraz, Tehran, Esfehan.
U is for Unlawful Acts.
U is for Unknown, all the Persian letters of the alphabet that never sunk into the whorls of my brain.
U is for the United States, forever entangled for oil and control.

V is for Victim
V is for Vexation, we are subject to the same imperial ills against our mental colonization.

W is for Wockner, Rex Wockner, the first journalist to reveal in 1990 the organized campaign of homosexual extermination the Islamic Republic of Iran planned in private meetings.

X is for the unknown, the women who weren't taught to read, who didn't know to write their love down, to find their self despite a beating from father, brother, or husband.
Y is for Yanni in chare michoni, you mean this is the work that you're doing? Writing?

Z is for Zeebah, beauty in all our ways.
Z is for Zenith, the highest point we haven't reached yet, for we have so much farther to go.

Vascular Roots

I wish someone told me
there was an in-between space
where desire lies hidden in plain sight

how your fingers hooked intertwined
with mine made my
heart palpate before I knew
the way a boy's lips felt
a tender glimpse of potential
wavering between two poles

cutting my teeth on kisses with
best friends, girls who I liked,
the flutter in my chest belying the
practiced intention for boys,
the elusive golden anointed ones

swept underneath, hidden, and
forgotten as your soft skin brushed
against mine, a chrysalis cracked open
too early
pupa ejected, splintered through the veins of my heart, scarred sinew
knitted over the darkness creeping inside,
tied up in an aortic valve, restricting breath and body

the way high school sweethearts bend
and grow around each, like an entangled
vine strings itself whorled over a tree
trunk, roots branching out underground
the concrete pavement poured over
sapling roots

defined by where my genitals smacked
months to years landmarked passage together
maidenheads shared, driving around a
suburban town suffocated under a blanket of bleach, graduation,
moving over a bridge golden
tree roots resilient in their growth,
lifting the concrete

the light breaking in between the slabs

yet I was hungry for
peach juice on my tongue
soft between my lips
still a spectator, not a participant
marking the way chasms cut,
painfully longing to be connected to
something larger than,
a difference in desire that set it all on fire

I broke, in a different way. Yet
you loved me, despite the pull
of my stomach in the direction of
an atlas uncharted,

as you disentangled your vines,
choking on the rot between us,
falling from my skin, butterfly wings crisply unfolding away from you,
trembling wet, drifting aimlessly
until I was drawn to the warm blaze exuding from a celestial sight.

there were stars in
the dust of your shoes,
with rivers of light
flowing downward as
you stepped towards me
I fell at your hips
Your iliosacral notch cupping me

Holding my breath feathering
against your skin.

Won't you walk the ventricles of my heart
to clear the darkness in my aorta, cleansed
giving breath to cells red and white

I feel you there
in the quiet thumping
in the contracting and
squeezing between chambers.

Leaves of Dissent

They call him a good Muslim boy,
On top of a tower, he calls men to prayer.
They don't know what unfurls
between the leaves of his Muhammad's words.

Between these book leaves,
expertly cut into the spine,
Lies Rumi, Marx, Hegel, Sartre.
Muhammad is his brother too,
 lowering sedition into their well.

The hummingbird truck comes
to fill their well.
Wets the ashes
of books that started revolutions
(but not this one).

He can't bring any books when he leaves. ones he spent his pocket
change on, Camus, Hafiz,
books he was beaten over,
soak up forbidden alcohol,
A falling
match
 Light the fires they jump over
It catches on the page
This is not a pleasure to burn.
Yet they are carried in his mind.
His blood.
Passed on.
For the love of literature is hard to stomp out
(like a communist manifesto,
or a silk road poem)
Years later, Sartre came back to him
 in the form of a child
 reading. Reading
 books.

Quinn Carver Johnson

Quinn Carver Johnson was born and raised on the Kansas-Oklahoma border. He currently attends Hendrix College where is pursuing a degree in English with a focus in Creative Writing and a minor in Gender Studies. He currently serves as the Fiction Genre Editor for *The Aonian*, Hendrix College's student literary journal. His work has appeared both online and in-print in various journals, such as *Right Hand Pointing, Broadkill Review,* and *Flint Hills Review,* with work forthcoming from *Dragon Poet Review* and *vox poetica*. He recently self-published a collection of poems entitled *If You Shut Your Eyes and Are a Lucky One.*

THE BLUE WHALE'S VEINS AND ARTERIES ARE SO BIG THAT A TODDLER COULD CRAWL THROUGH THEM WITH EASE.

After being swallowed by Monstro,
Pinocchio promptly drops to his hands and knees
and begins crawling through the beasts veins
and straight into his heart.
The whale does not sneeze out
the boy and his father,
instead he cries himself to death
and the three of them—
a whale with a boy in his heart
and the boy's father in his gut—
sink to the bottom of the ocean.

A YOUNG BOY FILLS HIS LUNGS WITH HOPE, HOLDS A DANDELION TO HIS LIPS, AND EXHALES THE FOLLOWING WISH:

"We must cultivate our garden."

-Voltaire

and there have been days
when I have denied myself
the things I know I need,
when I have sought from
the hands of others
the tender touch my own
hands cannot muster.

I have been known to let
flowers wilt into dust
on my desk. I, too, will
someday allow my body
to crumble into the atmosphere.

I have often plunged my hands
deep into this good soil
and pulled from it the roots
of flowers, mistaking them
for weeds.

There have been, however,
other days when I have
looked out the window to see
petals sprouting from
my earth, bees and

butterflies fluttering
in the skies.

I have never been known
for the greenness of
my thumbs and my
gentle touch is often
course and calloused,

but I will try always
to plant seeds in
your garden and in mine,
to grow from this
dirt the flowers

to gift to you—blossoming
beautiful in their existence
alone. I, too, hope to bloom
into a beauty that needs no
conditions outside of myself,
that needs no one else's love
to feel loved, to feel beautiful,

to feel alive and strong and
less like a weed sucking life
from good soil, to feel worthy
of the life I have been granted.

WHEN I DIE

A sign on the side of the highway says
"Wildflower Area: Only Mow in Fall"

When I die, waste no time carving
my name into stone. Spend no money
on flowers to leave at my grave
only to wilt and die too. Do not
look for me in a graveyard,
you will not find my spirit there.

Instead, look for me in the cornfields.
When the Oklahoma sun takes hours to set,
know that I am sitting on a hill, watching it
and smiling. Know my smile when you drive
down through the mountains and, finally,
the earth opens up,   stretches out
        for hundreds of miles.
Find my spirit in that good, flat land.

Find my spirit on a bicycle cruising
through a small town. Don't look for me
in crowded city streets.

Look for me in your schools:
I will be both teacher and student.
Look for me where people are still learning,
where people are still teaching.

Look for me where there are good people
doing good work—the kind of work
that must be done.

Look for me in roadside diners,
leaving a good tip, wishing I could afford
to leave more. Look for me in coffee shops,
laughing into the evening hours. Look for me

where people are singing the songs they wrote
and the songs they grew up on.

If you don't look for me, don't worry,
my soul will return to you anyway.
Just whisper my name into the sky and
let the cool breeze be my answer.
If you see a red bird, know it's me.

If you must bury me,
rest my body beneath
a patch of grass and
let the flowers grow.

POEM FROM THE CIRCUS

I am lost in the circus after dark, after all the fun
has been shuffled back into its cage by strong men
with whips and loud voices. I am a young boy, with
trembling knees, shaking at the thought of falling

from this tightrope;

I am so much better

————at falling.

EYE LOVE YOU

In a poem you wrote about the first time
we met you said that *our eyes stared
into each other* and, months later,
when I finally get around to reading it,
I can't help thinking about two giant
eyeballs with arms and legs staring
down a hallway into each other's eye—
or, maybe these two eyes each have
their own set of eyes and, in that case,
they are staring down a hallway into
each other's *eyes*.

I suppose that these eyes are supposed
to be us, in this hallway, staring into
each other—and if they are really
looking into each other then what
are they seeing? Are eyes still filled
with rods and cones when they are
not just eyes, but entire bodies? Which
is to ask, do two giant eyes standing
in a hallway that are meant to be us
standing in a hallway have brains
with which to think and hearts that
bleed and stomachs filled with butter-
flies and knots and swallowed words?

And I guess, the way you intended it,
these eyes are not bodies and are, instead,
just our eyes, and maybe this is no
hallway in the first place for these eyes
to stand in if they were ever meant to stand,
and this moment is filled to the brim
with passion and butterflies and
swallowed words and eyes that are gazing
into one another, two souls meeting

and I'm just making a joke out of the whole

thing, but baby, just imagine us, our bodies
replaced with eyes that can only stare, with
no mouths to talk, to kiss, speaking through our
shared gaze, the batting of eye lashes, in this
hallway, filled with no words, only a sea
of eyes and somehow, ours meet,

and isn't that the most romantic thing?

EVAPORAT ON

'm gone.
'm gone and 'm never
com ng back aga n.

That's all the note said.

And, after you were gone,
all of my poems didn't
read the same anymore.
There were no more eyes
sharing a loving embrace
from opposite ends
of a hallway because, now,
it was just a hallway, empty.
Something like this:

EYE LOVE YOU

an erasure
after your absence

In a poem you wrote
            you said that   *stared*
into   and, months later,

I can't help thinking about
        a hallway
or, maybe   two

        staring down a hallway into
each other.

I suppose that these
            hallway[s], staring into

 a hallway   meant to be
standing in a hallway have brains
with which to think and hearts that
bleed and stomachs filled with butter-
flies and knots and swallowed words?

And I guess, the way you intended it,
these are not bodies,
                    this is no
hallway in the first place
to stand in if they were ever meant to stand,
and this moment is filled to the brim
with
swallowed words.

Jessica Dickinson Goodman

Jessica Dickinson Goodman is a queer woman working in tech and politics in California and spending her off-time teaching workshops for women in STEM in West Africa and the Middle East. Her first job out of college was working with survivors of human trafficking, a difficult and inspiring experience that informs much of her poetry. In 2018 she was published in the *Oakland Review*, *RFD Magazine*, and her works were included in the *Geek Out!* and *Hashtag Queer* anthologies.

The Garden of Arden
After the Orlando Pulse shooting

I spent the last couple of days feeling   like
cannon fodder. I have never sought

out strangers wearing clothes and hair and wants
like mine in the heat-sweat of a gay club.

But I knew the men he killed; dancers laid   out on the tacky
ground; women's hair spread

out like blankets over blood; their phones crying   out families'
texts. His 'hunting rifle'   sights-up

my nape, my dyke-y hair. He scopes
my combat boots, my Pride flare hid in my

closet. When our bi-bard's Orlando fled   his brothers' rage he got a
found family,   a happy marriage to his fated sex.

But his brothers didn't pack Sigs MCX.

**On my way to the Middle Klamath River
In Siskiyou County**

I pass a rainbow built of water-trucks
beside I-5. Someone had lined them up
in pride flag order: primary colors
between orange-green-indigo-and-violet.
I'm driving through a county where Donald
J. Trump won the primary by eighty-two
percent. Bars don't fly bright rainbow flags here,
but neither do trucks fly the stars-and-bars.
My river guide works a water-truck up
the alpine slopes where fires sprint up to char
the forests' burning hearts. He's seen faces
of friends as their trucks tipped and rolled off cliffs.
My favorite city sunsets--red, yellow
blue--were from smokey northern wildfires' glow.

Advice

I was 14 when
my Baba said if she had a choice
she would go with girls
because girls are kinder
to go with

Spawn

When I was 22
I called the children
I might one day bear
"spawn."

I got married that year
so my mother started asking
hinting
like a call back to the rivers
of her birth

When I was 25
I lived in Seattle and people
worshipped salmon
waited and awaited them
like the Christ-child reborn.

Salmon spawn –
but so do demons.

Ripping a thing free of me,
bloody, bruised and pale –
body distended like in Alien –
its mouth screaming toothless the end of worlds,
or at least, my world
where I am the solo actor
on my stage.

Salmon die when they spawn,
rotting as they birth – demons inhabit those they would kill.

And now I might want to

spawn
and I love the word even more,
because it lets me wear my terror –
and a sense of wildness – and loss –

and supernatural awe –
and the miracle of creating –
something
unknown,
ugly
helpless as roe
and I can think it is beautiful
and I can think it is pure
but she won't be required to be.

My child can be evil,
my child can be weak,
my child can be ugly,
and red-faced,
and bawling,
and clutch in her fingers the end of worlds,
and she'll still be
my spawn.

The mountains we avoid

Monarch butterflies hang a left
over the Great Lakes
because a brief millennium ago
there was a mountain there.

I won't sleep on trains or
leave my drink unattended or
leave a cave after dark:
survivors refuse to die the same way twice.

The mountains we avoid
in our minds as they were given
to us by our mothers make sense to
our souls' kaleidoscope of butterflies.

Carolina BBQ is an African Dish

I'm eating tamales in Nigeria,
and my Hausa friend calls them moi moi,
but they're cornmeal wrapped
in banana leaves with
spicy chicken, just like at
the Oaxacan market down
rio de Monterey behind my backyard
in San José

I bite into sweet maize and hot chicken and flash on a future-past
where corn ears didn't cross from Caracas to Lagos stuffed in the
pockets of slavers, to where every Southern cook knows
catfish stew and BBQ came from here.
I wish tamales had come to Abuja like the recipe
for Chinese egg rolls that everyone has served our delegation
as fancy food every day I've been in Nigeria
homey and harmless and good.

I feel a tick-tick-tick under my
breastbone reminding me
I'm going home by way of England tomorrow
and reminding me
so I can never forget and remain alive that the hands that cooked
this meat have ancestors buried
in my Knoxville slave-'owning' ancestors'
backyard.

Again?

Started in the Manzanar parking-lot

Look: we were once a country of lynchings,
of strange fruit hanging down; fourteen year-old
Priscilla Presley under a husband
whose touch the law said she could not refuse.
Look: we were once a country of courage,
where brave braceros crossed over on the
American dream and raised free kids in
the glare of border lights; where Moms interned
in camps stayed up all night to cook the New
Year's mochi with pale stolen rice. They knew
that people bound together cannot then
be broken. When Trump twirls truth around his
ring finger, he forgets history. Back then,
so many fought back; and we'll fight again.

Grace Piper

Grace is a queer pal of color carrying their butch body through the Whitest city (Portland, OR). With a background in gender and queer studies, they're currently working in publishing teen activists, artists, and writers with the nonprofit they co-chair Toolkit Project PDX. Grace's poetry has been shared in local small press, taken them through many slam competitions, and has been featured in a Women and Gender studies research collection. They're favorite senses are taste and sight and work to bring elements of that into all their work.

Decolonizing

You reach between me and two hills grow around your hands.

I am busy getting unfamiliar with the way
my body
moves

except when it is bent around you And the crisp white of
your sheets has me tangled too. still don't understand these
parts of me
locating

every time you
touch My bones
are getting heavier-
- denser and

sharper

I feel the way you
and these hills are tugging.
You for the soft,
the hills for the sharp.
My skin pulled taut
from
brown to purple to white.

there's nothing for me to hold onto.
I wonder how much of me
is couched
and how much is just lost.
And I wonder when I will get to talk about it without the shame of
feeling it.

Wilting

theres a hole in your heart
where your brain
is supposed to be.

i hold it
up to the light
and watch it kaleidoscope,
watch the blood drain out.
watch it wilt in my hand.

the skin
doesn't

pink up,

like it used to.

i spread out your faint body
i reel,
weep,
for all
the parts neither of us will leave with.

all this grappling
is your becoming.

Bubble Tape, 2002

sun sulked into my room
pink and chewy, humming.
wondering what your tongue tastes like from the street.

I don't want to be longing,
I want to be moving.
There's something to be said for fighting
and then deciding
you don't want it anymore.

When I think of it,
thick in the back of my throat,
i know the best grief—
good grief,
goes quietly;
abruptly.

Hydrogen Peroxide

growing you me into you
ankle deep
gulping/wallowing/sopping.

crack me open find me you
into me
blue blood veins bursting with teeth
let you fester
in me
like a wound.

say out loud "it itches,"
it hurts,
healing hurt.
the itch you cannot scratch.

The First Sunny Day in Portland Since Last Summer and it Turns Out *They're Gay Bashing in the City Today

today
i am a new bloom.
teetered with sunlight and thanking god it isn't raining.
we smoke blunts one after the other
eat entire bags of candy
whisper with princess nokia
deny deny deny
skip the state of the union
eat more fistfuls of candy
warm my hands with a cup of coffee
but I smile and I keep it cheesing
walk to 7/11 to get 7/11 brand ice cream
with a plastic spoon
this as good it gon get
walk back to your apartment against traffic
blue canister of pepper spray
don't you be like the rest
am i home
am i home.

*they're translates to alt. right white supremacist group Proud Boys who bashed
16+ queer and trans folks in Portland, OR from February 8th-February
22nd 2019*

Trader Joe's Medium Roast Pre-Ground

5 new leaves beat through the middle of winter
we rip through cold like it was meant for us
toes tucked under
getting warmer and warmer.
we cuddle close
maybe because we might be in love
but also because i can't afford to pay for heat.
i give you a rock wrapped up in a box
tell you this poem is the distance from my heart to yours,
short drives,
sharing cups of coffee
i'll make the press today—
you make it tomorrow.
you kiss my ears goodnight and
i wake up to you singing.
i hope we hold hands until we don't want to hold hands anymore.
all 5 leaves unfurl even though it's January
so i kiss them (you) good morning, goodnight, goodbye.

Nyuma Waggeh

Nyuma Waggeh is a Gambian American immigrant. She is an Africana studies/ English major at Rutgers University. She is a recovering alcoholic who enjoys poetry, James Baldwin, children, & committing her life to activism. She identifies as a queer Muslim and intersectional black feminist. She believes in radical liberation through education and creative expression. They are an aspiring educator/writer and love flowers. Pronouns are she/they.

Nepa

There's always a price to pay for freedom.
She knew that, when she
drank me.
No one could have told her otherwise.
See, it's cyclical. The cycle of
Life/death/transformation.
I am the siren luring you into the pellucid waters
Coaxing you in for your sweet demise.
I can see you in my reflection, being
crystal clear has never stopped people
Who refuse to see the blinding truth.
Once you are awaken, you can never
go back to sleep.
She knew the price of what it meant to
drink me.
The wrath of a scorpion awakens inside
whoever consumes the elixir of Nepa.
I am the absolute power that drives you
Insanely mad.
I am the truth you refuse to acknowledge.
I am the key to salvation.
I am Kokou.
You called me, I
never needed you. You
needed me.
In the deepest parts of her crumbling heart,
She knew I could help her.
Once she became me, I could see
through her murky eyes.
And, I watched like a black panther nesting
Over the Baobab tree. Waiting.
My mouth slobbering of the warrior blood
of my predecessors.
There he was— the devil reincarnated to
humanly flesh. Sitting as if
he had not put his ferocious hands
around my delicate throat. I mean
her throat.

See, it took a village to raise
a savage
of man.
Any man that uses abuse as a form.
Of power (and calls that love), will always
crumble
  By the blinding light
I possess.
I walked over as if
I knew my reign of power
Would end with her.
I grabbed him with my glorious might
by his cowardly throat.
His screams of agonizing terror
invigorating me like
a breath of fresh air.
Hell has no fury against a scorned
Scorpious.
As, he laid crumpled on the floor
In the fetal position.
Walking away, to sit in the middle of
the village of massacres of women
who come to me with the gift of
crippling desperation.
See, it's cyclical. The cycle of
life/death/transformation.
I am the poison that
turned a village into a
bed of lotus.

Victima Querella

My chest/my heart/my soul has expanded,

even my father couldn't
keep this

victim

down.

The ruptures in my heart have been filled with *acceptio.*

Baba, even Allah can't save you from the wrath you imposed on
me—

Pray for forgiveness,

pray to her,
pray to me.

You need it.

IMAGOES

Part 1

Justice, a crimson morsel, blood of my ancestors *graciously* used as
icing—how bittersweet

And what a conundrum we have found ourselves in, to
*learn*what it means to be black in America **M**ay our
ancestors be with us in the land of the broken dreams &
the gilded innocence *they*wear

Eternity, is what this time on America feels like— is this what you
mean by the *Negro* problem still prevails

Society can never move forward from what *they* don't choose to
understand, how will we ever be free?

Baldwin, my love you've taught me so much about myself and
where I've come from, I can no longer hide from

A*place*/jail/mindset—the ghettos never did learn how to love us
yet, we loved her brutally

Love, seems to be the loaded AK-47 to the *loaded* race
question—we never needed an answer to **D**oes it not
seem so easy to love thy neighbor when I am the most
despised in the neighborhood? **W**hite people will never
learn who we are, you told me to accept them despite of
their inhumanity

In what form of love is this—I'm still trying to figure out
what it means to love the savage in me/them **N**ever be like
them—with love, you taught me to be authentic, be Negro, be
other, be queer, be great.

Part 2

James, when I am lost I talk to you like you're still here. I am exhaustingly tired, the cheap labor/the exploitation/the fetishization/the inhumanity of my people puts a taxing price on my soul. My hope is fleeting, I know how you feel. I remember when I met you 3 years ago. It was a white man who brought us together. He was kind—he saw the humanity in me, I saw his. Anyways, I felt like you were only speaking to me like a kind of Jeremiah. Coming to preach to me the tidings of truth and justice. Telling the truth has made me unpopular like it did you. To be queer and black in a family of heterosexuality and patriarchy has made it difficult to love my family. You have forgiven your father, maybe one day I'll get there. Just not today. Yet, the love we have given each other from my siblings have helped us survive the world, our parents, our troubles. *Love does not begin and end the way we seem to think it does. Love is a battle, love is a war; love is a growing up.* As, the oldest *we* get it to watch them grow up and form their own opinions to navigate through life. Yet, I am horrendously scared of what will happen to them. It didn't take until 30 to realize America never had a place for people that looked like us. I cannot save them no matter how hard I want to. Your hope in humanity makes me cynically optimistic, nothing has changed since you've been gone. Black bodies seen as menacing, savages, otherworldly we are dying everyday. They left us in the cities of destruction—we were meant to die, yet here I am. I have learned to cherish what it means to be a writer because of you— the power I hold to spread love, justice, and truth. I still want to run too—yet, we all know anti-blackness is universal my love. I know they are still trapped and they may never wake up. The questions that haunt you still haunt me at night—what will the state of America be if we never wake up? What will happen to us? I do not know, James. I'm sorry.

Mother and Child

You birthed

Me?
Do you not remember the brutal yet loving way you embraced Me?
You *raised*

me.
The trauma/the pain/the denial became a-part of my DNA.

Yet, mother never told me this monstrous black hole
would follow me since I was a child into adulthood. It would
get to know me, become the Best friend I never wanted—
know my hidden Quirks, make love to my fears and

never leave no matter how fast I ran.

I ran. I deflected. I hid. I looked for saviors in
everyone but me. I

discovered that lust and love were interchangeable if You
used it in the *right* sentence.

I ran, and keep

running. You keep finding me
Mother. No matter, who I sleep
with or under, here you are
Chastising me. Telling me
In the back of my mind I'm much more Than easy fuck and

settling for
boys

Who refused to ever learn how to grow

up.

Don't you think I know that?

Logically, I know that makes sense—it just doesn't add up.

And this is insanity. And this is insanity. And this is insanity. And this is insanity.

And this is insanity. And this is insanity. And this is insanity. And this is insanity.
And this is insanity. And this is insanity. And this is insanity. And this is insanity.
And this is insanity.

Mother *always* told me, that I can never love anyone until I learn to love myself. This has never stopped me Mother from— loving you while it kills me, selflessly saving others from themselves, and dying

A tolerable excruciating death so you can live.

I am alone amidst a village.

Mother never taught me
what it means to be part of a community. How to feel loved
Unconditionally in spite of—
myself.

Yet, I found you. A child just like me. We are broken & whole & alone & full of life

& sad & crazy & alive & stubborn & willing & honest & selfish & selfless. All at the same damn time. And just for today that is okay.

C. Thomas

C. Thomas has graced numerous venues. C has been featured at Studio 2001 Art Gallery, Busboys and Poets, Angelina College, Howard University, Eleanor Roosevelt High School and Journey of Faith United Methodist Church. Just to name a few venues and was named a Pioneer of Poetry by NUSPA (National Underground Spoken Word Poetry Awards) in 2015. Ever the advocate, C. Thomas continues to raise his voice through his art for the benefit of Child Abuse Prevention Awareness, Black Lives Matter, SGL (Same Gender Loving) and the LGBT community which he is proud to be a part. He knows there are many other minds, bodies, and souls to be touched by his message. C. intends to continue to challenge mindsets and command stages.

No Apologies No Regrets

Leviticus ch. 20 verse 13 says: If a man also lie with mankind, as he lieth with a woman, both of them have committed an abomination: they shall surely be put to death; their blood shall be upon them.

I never asked for this, in fact I remember trying to pray it away. Altar call every Sunday, laying my hand on the bible, making promises I wasn't going to keep to a man who was supposed to deliver my soul from sin. I taught myself to hate me, this wasn't normal behavior according to the masses. I was led to believe I was going to be a disappointment for the rest of my life; the shame I'd bring upon me and mine because of this lifestyle I'm living.

Sissy, punk, boy bitch, and faggot, slogans used by homophobes to advertise my sexuality and to bring attention to themselves because picking on the weak was one of the coolest things to do. Neverminded I was hurt or fearing for my life but as long as their homophobia reminded me of how they felt, then for them, all was good. I wondered what I did to deserve this. Was this my punishment for loving man? With everything I was going through, something had to give.

At the age of 16, I told myself (way before Lady Ga Ga did) I'm beautiful in my way. And no, God made not one mistake, after all I was made in his image. No more living in fear and being suppressed by the ignorance of others, my rainbow was glowed in all of its bedazzled glory and I accepted who I am.

Affirming my sexuality made my life easier. I had thicker skin for dumb remarks, refused to fuel the heartbeat of Homophobic America. Every day I found a new strength, because what doesn't kill you makes you stronger.

Twenty-two years later, I look back on everything I was told I wouldn't have or be because I'm living in sin. Aren't we all? How fitting to project their own flaws and insecurities upon me because they're miserable with their own. So it doesn't surprise me that my actions are still scrutinized because according to them I'm the root of all evil and the greatest abomination to walk this earth.

BUT....

Shout out to those who lie and cheat or beat on their spouse after taking vows in front of God to love and protect. Big ups to the priests molesting altar boys in the name of Jesus. Let the church say Amen! Warm welcome to the nuns birthing and killing off their offspring and funeralizing them under the church. Hallelujah!

So who are you to tell me I can't love a child and raise them in a stable home?......Crickets...... Who are to tell me I can't love my husband and grow old with him?......Crickets...... Who are you to tell me I can't have equal human rights because I'm gay? Boy you wearing skinny jeans sagging off your ass and screaming I'm a "G"! Crickets! At this time I say take a seat and have several.

Lawrence Martin

Lawrence Martin, is a writer and poet born in Austin, Texas, and raised in Houston and New Orleans. In youth, Martin studied ballet at Houston Ballet Academy, and piano under the Teltschik brothers. In 1966, at the age of 13, Martin came out to his very large Catholic family and to his friends at St. Cecilia's Catholic School in the Memorial suburb of Houston.

Martin has lived in Houston, Covington and New Orleans, Manhattan and Los Angeles and for the past 24 years has made his home in Austin. After a too-short career as a singer and dancer, Martin became a government procurement officer, but has never stopped writing.

Christopher Thomas No. 1

Because he did not know whether to kiss the man's forehead or his lips he kissed his own palm instead and touched it against the end of his world which was, that night, the doorway that separated that moment from a lifetime that would soon be separated by doorways and walkways and sidewalks and streets, highways and bridges, the faint smell of rain and gasoline and the fainter longing to have known the feel of that forehead or those lips.

He had never been this weak in youth. He knew instinctively that weakness was the province of age as sure as certainty was youth's best friend.

It wasn't fear. Fear had fled long before. Thin smoke from oncoming flame. It was that other quality of youth that was lacking now. Certainty. The certainty of shivering in cold or sweating in heat. The certainty of skies thick with clouds in spring and tumbling wind in early fall. The certainty that there exists a marked difference between forehead and lips.

How could he feel that difference now when he could no longer comprehend the difference between manhood and child's play, between desire and affection, between a palm-kissed door and lips as moist as whispered dream.

And it wasn't guilt. He couldn't remember guilt. He could remember the man's forehead and he could remember the man's lips. But not his own. Not anymore. And then he wondered: what exactly was love to be in old age? What to consist of, what to consist in? Should it imitate the fire that burns skin from the inside out? The heaving of flesh that urges itself into the life of another? The movement of breath that cannot be caught except inside a lover's mouth, or seized between his teeth or caught in the voracity of hair entwined in rough hands?

Not possible. Not anymore. That would be make-believe.

Guilt had more possibility for him. Guilt or fear. And neither had any possibility for him at all.

So he thought back. Not long back but some time ago. To other bridges, and highways, to other streets and lamp posts, and sidewalks, to the faint smell of rain-soaked gasoline, and to doorways and to one doorway in particular: the doorway that had opened on to the man whose forehead and lips he could not decide whether to kiss and, if to kiss, in what manner and with what thought? Wouldn't such a kiss - no matter to head or to mouth - soon need a hand in which to cradle one or with which to touch the other? He thought about this too and whether his old and thoughtless hands could shelter in a fabric-covered chest or stomach or waist. And he remembered these as well.

Not only these. No. But also the smile that broke his heart each time he thought to lose it. The arms that opened warm in greeting or folded tight across the unknown and now unknowable story of the man's life. The story, he thought, that is too short for me to hear and too long for me to do without hearing.

Christopher Thomas No. 2

How could I doubt that beauty lives and still may soar?

That skin may soften hearts and flatter by proximity?

Or form as lush as Spring may still excite?

Not so I think, when liquid eyes look back at me

From years long passed, and love once hushed

Now wails its memory aloft!

What invitation smiles a world beyond embrace?

Or hands, or brow, or fingers touch a chest

That held a heart and rendered there a life so bright

It now pronounces just exactly as before?

So long as you are somewhere on this earth

No longer Doubt but Courage is this age that quickens longing

Sure as death makes love immortal.

Christopher Thomas No. 3

I want to be that thoughtless, hungry man,

The one whose reckless brawn your fingers crave.

Or he whose muscled form your hand

Like master molds obsessions to enslave.

I want the flesh that stitches soul-to-souls

Your spirits bound then tumbled into dust.

And more: the sweat his breath controls

Surrendered now, and captive to its lust.

I want these things like men want life

Or folly's shill that turns to strife

And bates that one immortal Martial plea:

A man to every other, a boy, alone, to me.

Christopher Thomas No. 4

First love like nightmare wrapped in thunder

Drowned in pain but clean and soaked in Rage

Whose throat his words cannot expel

Nor skin his tattered youth shed off

Or eyes like flares his heart bleeds out.

Then warrior he, a rock he holds

In hands once soft as dough now rifle clad

And squinting at his Target though his mind

Could forget, could love again.

A knight emerges robbed of saber, bow and dagger

But not one has pierced his pounding vacant heart

Where Pain and Fear-bound Rage exalt

And then alone the man emerges.

Is courage born or only made

And who among us all should know?

And what the cost of love denied

To child, to warrior-knight, to man?

Silence all beneath a ghastly sky

Whose memories are cost enough

To pay for first love's birth again

Or quash a night-time's blackened Roar?

Randall Ivey

Randall Ivey writes from South Carolina and is the author of a
novel and three story collections. His work has appeared in
journals, magazines, and anthologies all over the United States and
England.

AUTOBIOGRAPHY OF A SINNER

I'm an old man now and plenty dirty,
A codger who still loves the cock
Of anyone eighteen and up
With a smooth hard body and a smile
From next door. The jock. The frat boy.
The escort. The stripper. The sullen punk.
The well-dressed Mormon boy. The waiter.
The clerk. The mechanic. The cook.
The movie star. The TV unknown.
The porn star. The wrestler. The politician.
I could take on a whole world of hard dicks
And never give up, never get enough.
I'd go anywhere, risk anything for a taste
Of male beauty in its stiffest form.
I've sucked off men in bathrooms,
In libraries, outside strip clubs,
Inside strip clubs, in motels and
Hotels innumerable. Hell, I even
Got a dude hot once in a Maserati
And finished him off in his kitchen.
I've tickled assholes with tongue
And with finger and once made a stud
In New York come *twice* by sucking his hole
And jacking him off at the same time.
(My mouth was a fucking suction cup on that hole.)
He squirted loads on my chest.
I jacked off a boy in a movie theater
After he'd done the same to me, getting me
So hot we eventually had to abandon the movie
And go home to finish our own scenario.
(It was *As Good As It Gets* playing, and Lord
Almighty the same could be said for Andrew's
Handjob. He had me screwed up so I tight
In my seat I felt tingles in all corners of my body.)

WHORE

...I'd be yours,
Kneeling before you
In happy abnegation
Of whatever it is
That makes me a man.
If I could, I'd give you
What it is you want:
A swollen pussy you
Could pound into dust.
"You don't need a pussy,"
An old beau once told me.
"You've got a big ass."
So I have an ass with its
Hungry hole and an even
Hungrier mouth and hands
That could yank strings
Of cum-pearls from you.
I'll squat, kneel, lie prostrate:
However it is you want
To take me, so long as you take me
And leave, after hard fucking,
Viscous trails here and here and here –
Chin and belly and lower back.

MIRAGE

The three of you shimmered into view,
A motley crew of three, blond, black, and brunet,
Circling the green heat of the small town campus
Like lost sheep but defiant in not asking directions.
I glanced at you quickly and threw up my hand
In hopes you might be prospective students
And end up in my classroom where I could,
Eventually, ogle and tease you as I do
Those young men whom I truly love.
But you did not see me or did not care.

Minutes later the rain came and you scurried
Car-ward toward warmth and safety.
I saw you piling into one vehicle
And at once a vision came of us conjoined,
One mass of brazen nudity, limbs working
Like gears on an all-male sex machine:
Me sucking you off one at a time,
You spanking my chest hard,
Reddening the nipples, taking them
Into your fingers, your lips

Shaking, pinching, sucking them,
As though I were a bitch from a porno.
Oh I want that same vulnerability,
With a ripe cunt to offer your cocks
Your hands, your frothing mouths.
I want to be the pussy for every
Hard-dicked college boy with
A beautiful smile and a smooth body.
I want to be the cum receptacle
For every turgid Ganymede on Earth.

REINCARNATION

Your stiffened prick
Winks with single drop
Of cum, which I'd gladly
Take into my mouth and
Bowels in hopes it might grow
Me into the same blue-eyed
Blond who now stands stiff
And lovely before me.

RUVIM

Like almost every man I've ever loved,
You simply disappeared one day,
Like so much ephemera or smoke.
I haunted the restaurant for weeks
Afterward looking, hoping for you.
"Ruvim?" I asked another boy.
He shook his head.
"No Ruvim. He's gone. I'm sorry."
And that was that. And suddenly
I lost my appetite for Italian
(But not for Russian.)
You were a bombshell the night
I wandered in with an innocent
Hankering for anti-pasto and red wine.
Hair scalloped smoothly from left to right.
A mite faggoty, but it did set off that firm jaw.
Lower down: the fuzz-glinting forearms,
The subtle rise of pectorals. Further:
Long legs encased in black dungarees.
You had hands that looked older
And more work-worn than a sixty year old's.
I watched them as they gave and retrieved
Platters to other diners, thrilled at the play
Of blue vein upon blue vein, of flash of joint,
Of dimpled fingers and moon-pressed cuticles.
I loved you at once without speaking a word
To you, and when *you* spoke, in a voice
Deeper than any hell of a Gulag,
Love cauterized itself to a beaten
And bruised heart.
I requested you each time I went back
And left you a generous tip.
For what? That you might love me?
Or at least never forget me?
But you left. Poof. Like that.
Now I must go elsewhere for Italian
And for love.

Corey Qureshi

Corey Qureshi is a queer writer and musician based in Philadelphia. Their writing is for and about queers working to exist under late stage capitalism. They read flash fiction for Homology Lit and help make Café Con Leche (@cafeconlechepress). You can find a list of finished and forthcoming writings at neutralspaces.co/q_boxo. You can find their face and words on social media @q_boxo

The Hourglass

To the side of the counter was an hourglass made of two glass jugs. The sand inside totaled roughly two hours. The store's owner, Antonia, made it one of the few days she spent in the store. One morning she presented it to me with a few rules.

"When you open up in the morning, get the hourglass going. Every time something interesting happens, reset it."

"Do I have to do it every time someone buys something?"

"That's up to you," she said. "I wouldn't. This place isn't sales driven. Either way, if the sand runs out at any point during store hours, you're welcome to close up and leave."

"Really?" I asked.

" I know you've got other things going on." She smiled. Antonia had always been super friendly to me. She didn't need anyone to run her store full of trinkets. It was a vast collection. There were carvings of all sizes, statues, crafts. She loved to collect art objects in her younger years. An expense account coupled with kleptomania built a mass of objects impossible to share living space with. After years of this, she decided a location for shedding the stuff would help. We vaguely knew each other and she heard I needed work, so she reached out.

It was another day, a slow one. I'd only flipped the hourglass twice so far. The first flip was the opening, the second a stack of manuals collapsing on their own. I started thinking it was just me, detached from the moment, not noticing much. The night before was another of sleep dodged hours staring into things barely remembered.

A young guy came in. He looked at me, turning quickly with a smile at my "hi". I tried dipping back into my book, but he was too beautiful to ignore. Bursting out of his clothes in a mix of soft and strong, hairy all over. The people in this town all looked the same, I was always a bit excited to see people with dark hair.

After doing a few things to distract myself, I looked back. The boy was putting a golden figure inside of his jacket. He turned, walking out of the aisle and away from the counter. At this point I couldn't look away. He picked up a small statue, came up to me with it.

"Hey.. How much would you ask for this?" He was fidgety, anxious to walk out. "Mmmm. I'd say six bucks." He reached down for his wallet. "Buuut. The gold piece in

your coat'll be thirty."

His cheeks darkened with embarrassment. "How'd you catch that?" He didn't try hiding the guilt.

"Stealing is pretty damning. You either do it or you don't. It isn't hard to watch, sweetie. You gonna buy it?"

"Nah, I don't think so." He made a move to go after putting it on the counter. It was funny to me how ready he was to ditch the figure. It was funny, and then it wasn't.

"Normally I wouldn't do anything, but your attitude's really rubbing me the wrong way." He stopped. "What did I do wrong? You still don't need to do anything." He looked

concerned, almost angry. Suddenly his expression softened with a snap in a way that made me jump inside my skin without realizing. His eyelashes lengthened in a way somehow accenting the moistness of his full lips. It was hot.

"What do you think of taking me for lunch then?" I asked. My heart raced in a way that made me question if I'd actually even asked. His smile grew slow and huge like I hoped he would be.

"I can do that. Where were you thinking?"

"Omar's," I replied. "I need soup on a day like today."

"Alright, so Omar's. Does an hour from now work?"

I looked at the hourglass. It still had a while to go, maybe an hour and a half. I thought for a second. "Yeah, that's fine."

He gave me the six dollars for the one piece he still wanted and left. I locked the door and changed the sign in the door's window to closed. I realized as I swept that I still didn't know the thief's name. I'd just have to remember the rare set of eyes that didn't look disgusted at me.

As I went to leave, I looked back at the hourglass. There was still something like forty minutes on it. I'd never left this soon and was on edge about meeting this straight guy. I thought of dashing back in to write a note of explanation just in case. Instead, I dashed back in and flipped the hourglass for the interaction I'd been caught up over.

I took my time as I walked down Erring Ave., headed to Omar's. I thought about the man I was going to meet. The way he was so quick to drop the thing he was trying to take still bothered me. Does he treat people that way too?

It'd happened to me before. Treated like a body with no being, discarded at the first sign of trouble. Having to even question this was a red flag, enough to make me change my route. At the next corner, I turned left instead of heading on straight to the cafe. I went home.

Andres Fragoso Jr.

Andres Fragoso, Jr., is an author, blogger, a freelance ghostwriter, journalist, poet, publicist, and much more. He is the author of "Listen, Poems on Being Gay, Bi-polar and Alive". Andres writes from the heart, from experience and from within with hopes and dreams. He volunteers his time as Secretary for The Henderson Writers Group. Loves to create new stories and has many ideas to write. In writing gay fiction, he shows the other aspects of being human in his works. Without dwelling on either issue, his characters come to life overcoming obstacles that are beyond their control. You can find his works at www.andresfragosojr.com

As Brave as Icarus

There was a time when I was free. Free from pain and deceit. So naïve in my youth, Jason the Argonaut had taken me as his lover. Life was eternal. The one with whom I would spend my existence. A castle he built for me in the clouds.

On our last night, he carried me to bed. Laid me on the covers, kissed my lips, with his tongue searched for my soul. Hovered over me and peeled my shirt off like I was a grape. Seductively and caringly. He leaned back and removed his shirt. Held my hands to his flat stomach for me to caress every inch of his torso. The morning light did not stop Narcissus from envying his beauty. Adonis himself would have killed to be as handsome. Muscular, hairy, warm. Each orange hair on his chest was mine to do with as I pleased. And I did.

"Stop pulling so hard." Jason stood over me, leaning forward for me to remove his belt and open the top button of his jeans and lower the zipper. Pulling his white briefs softly were stretched out the from pent-up energy held underneath them. A bright spot on white cotton marked the wet X of his excitement. I had to taste him. To feel him in my mouth. To sample his glory. I kneeled and caressed from ankles to knees appreciating every hair on his legs. Leaning forward to his knees I kissed my way up his thighs.

"Ohhh. I love how you tease me."

I arrived at the cloth barrier which hid his most prized possessions, a Phoenix laying two eggs. It was breakfast, and I was hungry. I sniffed my way up the stitches concealing him. I bit on the band and pulled down. As the barrier bent to my will, his Phoenix slapped my nose. Pulling his underwear to his knees and kissed the thigh that did not get my attention earlier. Reaching to his dark red nest, took one globe into my mouth and squeezed my tongue to the roof with it in place. I wanted to crack it open. After releasing it, did the same with the other.

"Ohhh. I can't take this…"

Pulling away my tongue rested on the base of Mount Olympus. Licking my way to the head of the gods and kissed the Ambrosia from the tip. Wanting more. Wanting his essence. Wanting to be his.

"Oh, yeah You're going to make me blush."

I didn't know what he meant by blush. I didn't care. I wanted him to gush on me, in me, over me. I held him in my mouth and gave a subtle squeeze with my tongue. His body reacted to it. I sucked more as I absorbed him inch by inch, taking my time. Letting my tongue massage from side to side. My lips tickled by crimson forest, with my throat I pressed him and eased back up.

Jason holds my head forcefully. "No. Don't stop."

He pulled me toward him until my nose bent with his stomach gagging me and increased the rhythm. I gasped for air. My eyes gushed tears of fear. The pleasure of him on my tongue and my throat became a pain. Needing him. Wanting him. I had to get away from him. Again!

"Ohhh. Don't stop. I'm going to co…"

A quick gush of Ichor forces its way down my throat. I tasted some as I threw up into my mouth. He didn't let me move. I forced myself to take as much of him as I could or suffer the consequences. I counted the times he climaxed. That time it was six, not his usual eight. But these were stronger, thicker, and with a much sourer taste.

"Good boy. Don't let go yet."

Jason pushed my head hard. I fall back on the bed. Laying on top of me, holding my hands over my head tightly and fell asleep. Loud snores kept me awake. A heavyweight on my chest prevented my breathing.

Months later the castle crumbled with his lies, his deceits, his fists and I fell hard to the earth. My pride wounded, my self-esteem lower than the ocean floor. My dream had crumbled. I was so afraid of men. I feared raised fists. I feared broken bones and purple bruises. I wouldn't wish hospital stays, months in comas, body casts to my worst enemies.

A fortress built on grounded deep in the earth and as high as the clouds. From my private prison, I saw the clouds above. A god in my own right. Up there nothing could hurt me. Not even Jason. In my hubris, I created a prison in my mind, my body, my soul.

Lonely, desperate, and depressed. This was not a life I wanted for myself. I searched for a man who believed in me, respected me, protected me from harm. A man who would warm me when I was cold. A man who would feed me when I was hungry. A man who would dry my crying tears.

Icarus. He was a healthy young man. Trapped in prison high up not on his accord. He died in his escape. Icarus was brave to take the first leap into the open and took flight. I was not as strong or courageous as Icarus. Staying alive. To have a life. Living with a man who would love me.

Fathering strength, gathering feathers of faith, the glue to bind me together. If Icarus flew from his prison so could I from mine. I stood at the top of my castle with the strength to soar.

Stepping into the open below me and flew to a happy place on earth. It was time to be a new person with no fears, with no set boundaries, and with set goals to be satisfied. My first flight in many years and I was gliding gently into the land of mortals.

"Come to me." It was the voice of Jason. How did he find me? I looked up and saw him. My Argonaut, my sun, my soul, my reason for being called me to him.

Slowing my descent to rise to the skies. "I can't. I won't. I'm going home."

"You want me. You love me. You need me. I NEED YOU."

Why me? What did I do to deserve this?

"I love you. I need you. I want you. Fly up to me and be mine forever. I will love you unconditionally."

"I'm coming, Jason, my love. Smile for me. I'll make you happy again."

"Up, come up. You will see and feel how much I love you."

What if I was as brave as Icarus? What would it be to fly close to the sun?

I hesitated. Jason had hurt me. I reached the Zenith. My hair burned. My nose bled. My breathing became shallow. Not again. I didn't want to bleed and not be me anymore. I couldn't take more of his love, of his devotion, of his pain. My body ached from the strain he caused. I didn't see anymore. I didn't feel anymore. I didn't care anymore.

I decided I wouldn't go back to Jason. I was a broken man as it was. And I wasn't starting over. No one wanted a damaged man. No one wanted someone left for dead. No one wanted seconds.

Suddenly letting myself go I began to drop, wax melting, leaving feathers in my wake like shooting stars. Each star a hope scorched by him. Each star a tear of pain caused by him. Each star a day in my life where he used me, broke me, bled me.

There had to be another way to find Elysium with a man that would love me for whom I am, and this was not it. Jason was not the one. I'm tired of kissing Lycia's peasants to end up with toads, and never find my Anteros.

A man took me to bed as his equal. I took my time removing his shirt, his shoes, his socks, his pants, and his underwear as I kissed every part of his exposed body. He removed my clothes, and we giggled like Plato's students who had discovered a philosophy.

Kissing, fondling, and wanting we fell into bed. We struggled to see who will be on top or the bottom. Finally, a decision made, and we got comfortable in each other's arms. Caressing, pulling hair, and squeezing every inch of our bodies. I kissed him tenderly. Laying him on his back, I kissed from his throat down to his navel. Leaving no exposed body part untouched. I kissed down to where his legs met and continued to his ankles. From there I pulled his legs over my shoulders and crawled towards him. I smiled deviously, and he blew me a kiss. My javelin waited for permission at the door of his most private place. A place never touched by man. A place I would call home. I pushed his legs forward a bit and gently entered him.

"Ohm." We said at the same time in different levels of pleasure. He welcomed me willingly. I gave into him lovingly. This is what love was about. We both moved, shifted, melded together in harmony until we climaxed. Easing out I laid next to him, he faced me, and in my arms, he fell asleep. I kissed his forehead and enjoyed how loving and trusting he was, and I would never break that trust. He would never be unhappy with me. Nor would he be hurt or in pain. That was my dream of love.

I wished for Semele's wish. I hoped for Elpis help. I prayed The Litai for a quick and painless death. I feared to hear my bones pulverize when I strike the ocean waves. He broke my bones, and nothing could mend them. Not even Eros could heal me. Nothing could bring me to love another man again. I would follow Eris from now on. Only she understood what I suffered. Only she could comfort me. Only she would hold my hand as she leads me to death.

Ogyges' flood expanded as Thanatos held my body. I gently floated like a skin on the waves, I sunk peacefully into the depths of the abyss. Air-bubbles rose as I violently imploded down to Poseidon's lair. A grain of sand made of a broken heart, an unfulfilled wish, and years of pain and abuse.

There was no rising from this fall. All the kind, loving, and faithful man have left with Ares to fight together in other battles. I remained in an eternal prison.

Knowing in my heart that I if I had flown to the Argonaut I would have died with the Sirens in his mind.

I had taken my leap of faith and kept my back to Jason. I refused to be in my prison or his anymore. I glided to the earth as the gentle wings caressed my body onto the tranquil waters of the lake. I rested on top of the waves. Breathing the fresh air, the pollen, and the green grass of life showed me that there's more to experience to be had.

This is not the end of it all.

This. Is. Not. The. End.

Isis Ramirez

Isis Ramirez has earned her bachelor's degree in English from the University of Central Florida. She is a blogger and content editor at lovepainandpoetry.com. Her blog memoir, "The Reflections of An Anxious Woman," has been featured on lovepainandpoetry.com and on Apple News. She is currently a freelance writer and aspires to be an English, and literacy, teacher in education nonprofit organizations. She is also obsessed with tea mugs, gender studies, *Shark Week*, and the ocean.

Dear Liz,

It's been twelve years since you smoked a Black & Mild in front of your Long Branch house. I told you it was no good for you, but you laughed it off and said, "shut up, Alexa." I wish I could have caressed your Salvadoran hair, while we watched your mother chop some *chicharrón y queso blanco*. Liz, I was a 16-year-old coward who hid your photos on my Motorolla Razr because I didn't want *mi abuela* to know that I had a shorty from New Jersey. Remember the first time we had phone sex? You moaned Alexahh, Alexahh, like Prince. You screamed louder Alexahh. Louder Alexahh. But my hands stapled my lips, sealed-shut like safes. Liz, I'm sorry

I pressed the red-dial tone. I'm sorry I turned on *South of Nowhere*. I'm sorry I raised the television volume to sixteen. I'm sorry I switched my phone to vibrate. I heard footsteps in my parents' kitchen. I saw my father by my bedroom door. I couldn't phone-fuck you in peace. I couldn't cum on my sheets. I faked orgasms from men who banged their thumbs against my clit during our one-month anniversary. Liz, I'm now a 28-year-old fresh out the closet *mami*, who searches for your AIM screen name. I prevented *chanclas* from being thrown to my head until my head was straight. Yet, why the hell do I still feel dizzy from a shot of *Patrón* and Anna

backing that ass on my lap? Liz, Anna sinks into my inner thighs. I grab my iPhone 7 on my dresser. Tongue in, I open the Facebook app and search for Elizabeth Martinez. I moan Liz, oh Liz, hoping to find your soccer jersey profile photo. Tongue out, petty-lust-smacks, Anna clips her bra, like Ziplocs. She spits out *jugo de Alexa* in my bathroom sink. Liz, it's been twelve years since you smoked a Black & Mild in front of your Long Branch house. I wish I picked the staples off my lips, and bled-out Liz, oh Liz, *te quiero para siempre.*

- *Tu Salvadoreña,*

Alexa

Brooklyn-Bamboo

Brooklyn-Bamboo,

do not jump off the Brooklyn Bridge. French

kissing Faye in your junior dorm room is not

a sin. French kissing Fen in the handicap stall

of Webster Hall is not a sin. Their tongues

blossom your Flatbush stalks.

Brooklyn-Bamboo,

do not jump off the Brooklyn Bridge. Eating-

out Ella under your shower head is not a sin.

Eva massaging your shoulders with avocado

oil is not a sin. Grow in your Flatbush pot

beside your high-rise window.

Brooklyn-Bamboo,

do not jump off the Brooklyn Bridge. The

East River will slit your roots. The East

River will mash your Flatbush leaves. The

East River and mother Mary calls for your

baptism.

"Come, my bamboo child, rinse off Eve's scratch

marks. Let the devil devour your strap-on. Come,

my bamboo child, intertwine your branch around

John's hips and produce an offspring. Come, my

bamboo child, sink into Straight-Hood. Sink, my

bamboo child, sink."

Brooklyn-Bamboo,

do not jump off the Brooklyn Bridge. Brooklyn-

Bamboo, blindfold your Flatbush ears. Brooklyn-

Bamboo, blindfold your Flatbush tears. Brooklyn-

Bamboo, the East River will not nourish your

bamboo tattoo.

Miss Sugar Shack

Miss Sugar Shack enters the Studio Museum in Harlem.

The breeze from the AC blows against her spring dress.

Miss Sugar Shack admires an Ernie Barnes painting, *The*

Sugar Shack, sistas and brothas who sugar shacked at

Durham Armory. From the corner of my eye, Miss Sugar

Shack notices my *I Want You* CD. Her ankle boots clink

against the floor. Miss Sugar Shack shacks her way towards

my CD, pulls it out of my paper bag, and hugs it against her

chest. Miss Sugar Shack, how long has it been since you

shacked on a sista? Miss Sugar Shack, how long has it been

since a sista wanted you the right way, like Marvin Gaye?

Miss Sugar Shack smooches the "After Dance" track, Miss

Sugar Shack places *I Want You* in my hands. Miss Sugar

Shack takes out her sharpie from her *Taíno* purse, Miss Sugar

Shack sketches her digits on my arm. Miss Sugar Shack writes

her chorus, *te quiero. Te quiero ahora. Ven, a vivir conmigo*

mi Ángel Morena, in Dominican-cursive like Julia Alvarez.

Traces of brown-heads, traces of brown-asses smear my elbow.

Miss Sugar Shack traces S-a-l-o-m-e U-r-e-accent n-a on my

shoulder. Miss Sugar Shack whispers, *"Como la poeta,"* as she

shacks her way out of the Studio Museum.

- Our chorus,

te quiero. Te

quiero ahora. Ven, a vivir

conmigo mi

Ángel Morena. I want you.

I want you now. Come, live with me my

Dominican Angel, immerse in a sista's

vulva at

Durham Armory.

The South Bronx *Reina* in Central Park

In Manhattan, N.Y. — She was walking behind a *Latino*, who didn't slow down for her at Central Park. She stopped and saw a Vicci Martinez portrait. The *Latino* didn't even dare to stand by her side. The *Latino* never wanted to know her favorite artist. The *Latino* never asked if she painted her bruises with acrylic paint. The *Latino* dragged her around like a plastic bag. Pathetic.

She walked by my bench. She paused. Her eyes lit up when she saw the cover of *Borderlands/La Frontera: The New Mestiza*. She bit her bottom lip. As I turned the page, I raised my eyebrow. Her breast aroused. The *Latino* continues to walk on by, like Aretha Franklin.

She peeped my lesbian-stud game, a pair of Converse, a long-sleeve Polo, skinny jeans, and a New York Yankees dad hat. I looked up and smiled. Her breast aroused. To my right, the *Latino* stopped walking half a block away. She looked to my right and bit her fingernail. She pulled out her mini notebook out of her back pocket.

She scribbled her Facebook username. She folded the paper in half, and said, "I saw you fold the corner of your pages. Do not ruin a good book from where you last left off." She handed me my new bookmark. The *Latino* was standing a few feet away. The *Latino* scrolled through his phone.

"Thank you," I said, although I knew she was playing it safe. She rushed to her *Latino's* side. The *Latino* grabbed her hand, a typical *Latino* technique to claim any shorty in New York City. Give the *Latino* another two blocks, and he will let go of her hand, like Rose did to Jack.

Her name was Alejandra Arana, a twenty-seven-year-old South Bronx native, who resided in the Upper West Side. Alejandra was a writer and painter. According to a *New York Times* article, Alejandra's boyfriend, Mateo Cruz, grabbed her by the neck, thrusted her against the wall, and choked her to death.

Alejandra, why you dated a bum ass *Latino* nigga from Harlem? Alejandra, you dope ass talented *reina,* why didn't you messaged me back that one night when Mateo kicked it with his *moreno* homies in front of Madison Deli? Alejandra, why couldn't you call me on Facebook audio? You always typed: "I can't Netflix and chill tonight. I have to cook *chuleta y arroz.* It's Mateo's favorite dish."

You always typed: "I can't meet you at Henrietta Hudson because Mateo wants me to iron his clothes before he goes to work." Alejandra, I didn't know I would type my last message on the night of Jan. 14, 2019. I didn't know that when I pressed send, your foot dangled above the floor. I didn't know that when I pressed send, you gasped for your last breath.

Alejandra, you were a good book that was ruined because Mateo folded the corners of your neck, all because of an overcooked *chuleta*. Pathetic.

Alejandra, two weeks ago you wore a long-sleeve dress, stockings, and high heels. You walked behind a *Latino* who didn't slow down for you at Central Park.

You stopped by my bench and bit your bottom lip because you knew it was the last day you will see your Vicci Martinez portrait, a lesbian-stud who sat on a bench, and wore a long-sleeve Polo, skinny jeans, and a New York Yankees dad hat.

Forever your Bookmark

Index

- The poem "The First Sunny Day in Portland" by Grace Piper (pg. 91) contains a reference to the Princess Nokia song "Bart Simpson"
- The poetry by Dena Rod (pgs. 58-65) contains information and terminology which has origins linked to the following sources:
    - Gharavi, Tina, director. *Mother / Country*. Frameline, 2003. Film.
    - *Hasha: A Newsletter by and About Iranian Lesbians/gays/bisexuals = Hāshā.* San Francisco, CA: Hasha, 1994. Print.
    - Kugle, Scott A. *Homosexuality in Islam: Critical Reflection on Gay, Lesbian and Transgender Muslims.* Oxford: Oneworld, 2013. Print.
    - Murray, Stephen O, and Will Roscoe. *Islamic Homosexualities: Culture, History, and Literature.* , 1997. Print
- "Go (an erasure of "Tango: Maureen" from Jonathan Larson's RENT)"

"Tango: Maureen" is the infamous lament in the musical *RENT* in which Maureen's former lover, Mark, and her current partner, Joanne, commiserate about their shared experience Maureen's infidelity. Notably absent is Maureen's side of the story, and this poem seeks to reclaim that moment.

- "Princess Bubblegum and Homura Akemi Advising the Author on Worldbuilding"
    - Princess Bonnibel Bubblegum is the monarch of the Candy Kingdom in the animated series *Adventure Time*. During the series she often clashes with former "best friend" (later revealed to be ex-lover) Marceline the Vampire Queen. This poem takes place during the *Elements* miniseries and the recounting of this period by Marceline in the episode "Ketchup," in which Princess Bubblegum is transformed into a tower of candy.
    - "Let Me Call You Sweetheart," written by Beth Slater, is the song sung by Princess Bubblegum in the episode

"Hero Hearts" and "Skyhook II" that transforms
beings into candy people.

- ○ "You recall their hair smelling exactly of a campfire"
  Marceline is tranformed into a candy version of herself,
  Marshmaline the Campfire Queen, which we learn in
  the episode "Ketchup" is by choice.
- ○ Homura Akemi is a main character from the magical girl
  anime series *Puella Magi Madoka Magica*. This poem
  takes place during the movie *Rebellion* in which Homura
  discovers she has become a "witch" (an evil being who
  uses illusions to trap humans) but cannot bear to be
  healed by her best friend, Madoka, as it will mean their
  eternal separation.
- ○ "anyways for when God has their bad days" In the initial
  series Madoka ascends into literal godhood, protecting
  all magical girls in their final moments and preventing
  them from becoming witches.
- ○ "than allowing a red inch of regret to bloom" In *Rebellion*
  Homura's witch form, Homulilly, is surrounded by red
  spider lilies, also known as Lotus Sutra and are
  associated with death and funerals.
- ○ "all the clocks of truth" Homura's initial magical girl
  power is freezing time briefly
- ○ "If entropy is inevitable" In the series an interfering alien
  race known as Kyubey decide the solution to the
  eventual heat death of the universe is creating magical
  girls that become witches when they despair.
- ○ "Love to/ you takes the shape of a frightening color"
  Homura's soul gem transforms into a never before seen
  shape after she kidnaps Madoka for her own. When
  asked what the new object represents if not a curse, she
  replies "It is the pinnacle of all human emotion. More
  passion than hope, much deeper than despair. Love."
- • "this morning i re(-)collect the sky"
  - ○ " sky/ planet's shift" At the time the planet Uranus, also
    known as the sky planet or sky god, was moving into a
    different astrological sign.

ABOUT THE AUTHORS

The Authors and contributors contained within this book can be found @imagoes_ on Instagram. Their bio's and more content about their thoughts on Queer poetry can be found at:

LOVEPAINANDPOETRYPUBLISHING.COM